I0483922

The Funny Side of Management

Vol. 2

Ethics

By

Ramaswamy Thanu

Printed by CreateSpace
An Amazon Company

Contents

I. Vanishing Ethics

II. Corrective Action

1. Vanishing Ethics

1. Cheating Game?

For ages business has been in existence. It is an essential commercial activity producing and providing goods and services of use to the community. It has all along earned respect. However, there are some aspects, which some business manifest through their activities and products, which cannot be accepted as desirable and socially beneficial. It is useful to consider some of these aspects with a view to understand the implications and how best the business community can overcome them or at least minimize the impact on the consumers.

Exorbitant Profit

No doubt business needs to be motivated. So profit is a must for the survival and growth of business. But it should not be the only motive. There are other aspects like customer relationship, consumer service and customer satisfaction that are important and necessary. The consumer has to be protected consistent with the stature, strength and standing of the business.

The balance sheets of many companies show high profits. If they pass on a portion of such profits to the consumer by way of price reduction and set apart a sizeable portion for community development it will earn goodwill and benefit both. Some companies are doing this. But business can do something more to alleviate the sufferings of the poor and less fortunate sections in society. This aspect has to be addressed seriously.

Pricing

There are organizations fixing price of the products based on what the market can bear or on the principle of exploitation. Many companies display prices on the wrapper and the markings are very high. This is seen from the heavy discount later given to the distributor and the customer. Often only a portion of the difference s passed on to the ultimate beneficiary. This may be justified as a strategy to boost up sales. But if they believe in customer satisfaction and developing a wider customer base there is justification for lower price markings so that the customer friendly approach of the business is transparent. There are organizations, which adopt 'Wilkinson sword' policy in relation to customers. They can afford to be less greedy and share the profits with the community.

By reducing costs business can pass on the benefits to the consumers and conserve resources. Many organizations pad up costs which could be cut down and savings attained. Such savings could be shared with the consumers.

Underweight. This is another form of refined cheating. It is a customer unfriendly act. No business can thrive on this policy for long.

Quality

There are cases of companies supplying substandard items diluting quality to gain short-term benefits. By and large most organizations adopting modern management practice improve quality and give importance to customer satisfaction. Those not in that category can definitely come up and make a significant contribution to the community by improving quality of goods and services.

Packaging

The objective of many a business seems to invest in packaging to make it very attractive to entice the customer ignoring the concept of value analysis. Such packages are half empty and hollow. The contents do not occupy even 70% of the full capacity and 50% of the cost. Because of this substantial erosion of consumer purchasing power takes place. Why should packing be made so attractive incurring huge cost? This drains away the resources of the company as well as that of the consumer. Is it not possible to reduce the cost consistent with market acceptability? If this is inevitable for satisfying, 'vanity buyers', then why not introduce cheaper packaging for budget consumers. Their resources will be conserved and put to better use.

Ethics

We often we find unethical practices in business. Unsolicited marketing techniques and exaggerated claims of advertisements are examples of this marketing disease. Businessmen can imbibe and introduce values in their business. This will definitely reflect in the overall growth of business in the long run. If a business does not grow in the long run despite having such a value system, the alternative is not to prop it up with unethical practices in pricing and quality. It is advisable to bury such business and diversify into another line of use to the community and the organization.

Products are dumped on the consumer exploiting the latter's gullibility. Business should educate consumers by giving right information about the products. They should not leave the exercise to be done by research organizations that do a useful job but after much havoc is done.

Social responsibility

Business will serve society better if it adopts a small area around its location for improvement of quality of life with focus on the poor sections of people.

Positive answers in the areas mentioned above will determine whether a business is rendering a useful service or sliding towards a cheating profession. Business can render better service if these adverse trends are reversed and the benefits passed on to the consumers. It will help to establish and strengthen good customer relationship and consumer base for mutual benefit. Let us hope business that by intention or accident slip into the trough of deceptive practices, realize the pitfalls and improve to serve the community and themselves better.

2 Vanishing Business Ethics

Are there Managers who have a soft corner for unethical practices? Are there in this world businessmen adhering to I values in the transaction of business? At a time globalization is moving at a rapid pace erosion in ethics is also rearing its ugly head everywhere. Unethical practices prevailing in one part of the world get transmitted to another part easily. Either no lesson is leant for corrective action or the nefarious/shameful practices are imbibed and this goes on .It subscribes to the belief that business has become synonymous with duplicity and deceit. Enron and Anderson revealed how mega corporate frauds are encouraged and executed. The result is business catastrophe. The business community globally should think over these setbacks and find out a lasting solution for restoring credibility in their operations and philosophies. If this is not done the incentive for upholding ethical values in business will dwindle. Firms strictly following a code of ethics will be at a serious disadvantage and they will pull down their shutters due to inability to face unhealthy competition.

Many firms strive hard to make quick money and to earn name and fame. They adopt unethical practices to boost their business temporarily. While they rise sky high they also crash land with a greater velocity making recovery impossible. Millions of shareholders lose, financiers incur heavy loss and society is impoverished. The promoters lack basic qualities like honesty, integrity, and respect for facts, and cordiality in relations, concern for right accounting practices. Products of poor or substandard quality are produced and distributed. Extortionate price is charged. Advertisements endorsing excellence of the product are grossly exaggerated-. Delivery schedules are not observed. There is a decline in the performance level. . Delivery schedules are not observed. False accounts give a distorted picture of finances and profits mislead shareholders and the public. Excessive prices are charged. They include many hidden costs. This is true in the case of services. Recruitment practices smack of unfairness in terms of salary fixation. Cash payments are demanded for posting. Government regulations are violated. Pollution control measures are not implemented in the case of food products, pharmaceuticals and chemical products. Measures for employee health and safety are inadequate and protective measures are absent. Many firms want to secure orders by bribing. This assumes huge proportions boosting up the cost of services. They collude with key officials to gain entry for their products at the cost of quality and competitive advantage. The result is consumer tragedy. The consumer is compelled to bear the brunt of this abominable approach. There are cases of meeting demands of corrupt elements in the government. Additional cost is incurred in various ways and the opportunity for supplying the product at a lower price to the customers is lost. Take the case of a Revenue Service official with "elastic conscience". He identifies a few rich taxpayers, meets them offering illegal concessions and relaxations. In return he demands services and perquisites, which involve substantial cost for the tax assesses. The latter by force cook up the accounts. When such accounts are presented the profit in the balance sheet dips and sometimes this becomes a loss. To window dress the balance sheet the company cooks up the figures resorting to unethical practices. One interesting case relates to a public limited company. It wanted to accommodate the funeral expenses of one of its directors in company account. It included $10000 under the head Packing and Forwarding. It was accepted. The deceased was probably packed and forwarded to heaven or to hell as the case may be! In another case a company paid a hefty bribe of $20000 to a government official. This could not be shown in the accounts statement as bribe. The management included it under the head business promotion expenses. This was disallowed. Actually it was given to the tax department in return for a promise of a lower assessment of tax. The company wanted to be honest but the tax official demanded it. So the company had to succumb and devise ingenious ways of accounting the expenses. There are innumerable instances of diluting ethics. The corrupt practices initiated at one end whether it is on the part of the officials or the companies, set in motion a chain of actions involving and breeding unethical practices. By imbibing a value system in the organizations and in government, such unethical practices can be reduced if not done away with. It is the responsibility of every citizen to make an earnest effort to imbibe and introduce a value system, which will promote business ethics .Let us all make a sincere effort towards this laudable goal.

3. Holistic Cheating

With the advancement in knowledge in every sphere of human activity and growth of civilization we also find many cases of fraud and cheating in business as if it were a profession of its own. Measures to curb this trend by governments and trade bodies have not produced desirable results and impact. This is brought about by individuals who enter business in the garb of entrepreneurs eclipsing ethics and forgetting social objectives. Let us consider some aspects of these unethical trends in business.

Some entrepreneurs are adepts in introducing this approach right from the start. Greed dominates their objectives. The project is copied from somewhere and costs are inflated. They submit a project proposal with rosy picture of cash flow and profits and influence the financial institutions to sanction funds. They meticulously knock off concessions and incentives offered by the government. This situation prevails in some countries.

They cleverly manage and ensure that their stake in the business is negligible compared to the total project cost. For example, a fake entrepreneur comes with a request to prepare a detailed report to knock off 50% subsidy towards project proposal preparation. He makes an interesting offer to the consultant to hook him. He wants a report with a receipt for the full amount of the project consultancy fee. With the receipt he goes to the financial institution and manages to get 50% of cost. He is gracious enough to offer 50% of the amount thus received, to the consultant. The latter also becomes a party to such fraud. Thus a chain of frauds is planned and often successfully executed. The businessman sets the standards which become precedents for others. When many fake entrepreneurs embark on such ventures the result is that the nation is silently looted. Many industries are over financed and ultimately they fall sick and enter the verge of closure. Part of the funds thus diverted is siphoned off for personal uses including building personal assets. The project becomes non-viable and falls sick. It fails to service the loan installments which fall in heavy arrears. It becomes sick though the promoter is prosperous.

In a frantic attempt to make good the loss and to hold on to the ground the business lowers the quality of its products, raises price, and adopts other dubious methods including short weight of products, raising false insurance claims and lowering of product quality. These steps bring loss of customers and goodwill. The business also resorts to collect funds for appointments of personnel. When it is unable to get the right personnel it resorts to fixing square pegs in round holes and looks for crooks who are given premium posts with wide powers for producing results regardless of methods adopted.

The business resorts to "suitcase culture" by which high denomination currency notes are filled in boxes to be gifted to decision making officials. It is a most effective way of lubricating decisions in some cases. Experts are engaged for this special purpose and high sounding designations are given to them on condition they fulfill the mission. The list is only illustrative.

Other measures adopted for deriving short term gains are purchase of substandard machinery and extravagant unaffordable personal expenditure. This results in working capital shortage, rising overheads and adverse health of the unit. But such a business collapses though the promoter prospers.

There is limit to which the government can curb these activities. Businessmen and trade bodies can make an earnest effort to improve the situation and bring about great relief to the customers and to the businessmen themselves through introspection and a philosophy of business culture based on values.

4. Deep Pocket Management

Management is a creative subject with tools and techniques for lifting an alert executive to attain professional excellence. While the skills are generally used for attaining core competence, there are also individuals parading as executives who make use of the managerial skills to enrich themselves. They become specialists in their field of activity and are liked, loved and worshipped by like-minded individuals. For relaxation and fun we shall consider a few cases of persons who fill their specially designed deep pockets with cash by sophisticated inventory mismanagement practices.

Any commercial activity is enough for them to follow scrupulously the operating philosophy of deep pocket filling. One example lies in the area of purchase. The key official may not be the person who is head of the department. Knowing that there are stocks to last for months or years, he places orders for huge quantities when sales representatives visit him. First his pocket is filled and any overflow will fill a brief case and the order is executed. The official prospers whereas the organization plummets.

Years ago such creative buying practices of some officials in an organization resulted in shoes for field staff adequate for 800 years considering the annual usage rate. If one area is plugged another window of ingenuity opens. For example while estimating material requirements, instead of the normal scrap allowance of 2% for copper the deep pocket official takes it liberally at 8 or 10%. So when 102 tons are to be ordered they order 108-110 tons. The extra quantity is a cushion available for receiving kickbacks and siphoning.

Deep pockets are filled to the brim and any overflow finds its way to bags and briefcases. They immediately organize country wide or even world tours to deflate the briefcases and inflate their importance.

In another case electric motors in stock were enough for the next 60 years considering the consumption rate. No wonder such organizations blocked huge funds in inventory, paying heavy interest to banks. They couldn't take delivery of essential materials worth one-tenth the value of the excess interest burden. If you ask them why this disease prevails the quick answer will be" that is the tradition and we don't want to be exceptions".

This phenomenon continues in organizations where there is slackness in control and the managers at the top level are not aware of what is happening. Examples vary from organization to organization and the extent of the loss and leakage is one of degree only.

We hear a funny defense from such champions of this deep pocket philosophy. They say 'old is gold' and that the sale value of such items later will be higher. This has helped some organizations to make profit without operations. They sell the material at high prices and make a surplus. The company may lose but the officials flourish. Surprisingly such persons are considered to be result oriented efficient executives. They are in great demand elsewhere where they find greener pastures and glorious opportunity for growth. For them deep pocket enrichment is part of ethics.

5. Hidden Technique

Management is the art of attaining definite objectives often with inadequate resources. Several concepts, tools and techniques have been evolved and practiced. But these techniques fail and surrender before a technique, which succeeds remarkably well. This is not taught in any B school, but widely practiced underhand. It is the technique of bribing. There are several ways in which bribe operates. We can take the example of cash payment. Where established techniques fail bribe succeeds. This raises the question whether it should be elevated to the status of a result oriented management technique.

Managers emphasize on results and that which produces results is considered the best technique or practice. This is similar to what Alexander Pope said," For forms of government let fools contest, what is administered best are best".

Bribing spreads its tentacles in all areas of economic activity .It has a comprehensive coverage. People in all walks of life sometime or other face this demon. It overpowers many. Often it is a hefty phenomenon filling deep pockets and large suitcases. Businessmen invariably keep this in their armory when all other techniques fail to get results. Even a simple decision without any favor invites bribe just because of the powerful position held by decision maker. Without this the decision will not be forthcoming or it will be unfavorable. We will consider two cases here where all techniques failed and bribing succeeded.

In one case a large company faced a strike situation, which they wanted to avert. The dispute was over salary revision and bonus payment. Negotiations went on for two weeks. The stalemate continued. The best human relations expert was brought. He analyzed every bit of information and negotiated presenting all facts. But the unions refused to be convinced and turned down the proposal. Then as a last resort someone suggested to try the hidden technique from the armory. He said, 'you bribe the union leader. You will succeed and the strike will be called off.' The management heeded the advice. Negotiations with the leader took place. These were confined only to the rate to be paid to him and not any of the technicalities of the agreement or wage revision. The leader gave a compromise formula which worked. The management was surprised. They had originally agreed to pay more but the unions were adamant and did not accept. Now even considering the bribe paid to the leader as a cost the total financial commitments were less. Not only this, the strike was called off. So bribing succeeded when expertise failed.

In another case one company got a bulk order for supplying 200000 tons of cement. The best marketing expert was commissioned and the most competitive rate quoted. The tender was rejected. Another company quoted higher rate but resorted to a hefty bribe to the deciding authority. It got the order and the technique proved successful. In both these cases modern management concepts and techniques failed but bribing succeeded with least effort and time. It needed only contact with the right point. But finally the order volume more than made up for the additional cost of bribing which was treated as part of business promotion expenses.

Considering these two cases and several thousand similar ones, are we justified in declaring bribing as a result oriented management technique? This is not taught anywhere, not even in B schools. No school or organization will openly advocate this technique for it involves ethics. But in reality it works whether it is procuring cement or ships, setting up textile mills or buying aircraft. Bribe Management deserves to be treated as a specialized subject for B schools! Ultimate success depends on how one succeeds in this game of bribing. Those who cling on to core competence and ethics will be drowned in the sea of bribes, which make organizations float, navigate and succeed. So you decide whether bribing should be elevated to the status of a result oriented management technique or not. If we believe in ethics and if B schools have to give importance to ethics then value systems should be introduced in business and bribe which is another name for greed should be eliminated .It is greed that foments and breeds bribe. When the question as raised before a CEO of a large Company, he said," My dear Gentleman, you have to treat it as cost." Of course it is hidden cost and a technique too!

6. C-Governance

We hear a lot about E- governance these days. But how many have come across C -governance. While the former is governance by adopting electronic means of communication, the latter can be taken to mean governance by corruption. Though no government openly admits this, the fact is that it exists and grows. The result is that the citizens suffer mentally and financially while the officials becoming prosperous. We have some examples to understand how this type of governance works and how sanity and fairness are discounted in favor of dishonesty and duplicity.

Corruption and greed dominate most of the democracies in the world. Even for discharging normal duties, officials who draw salary from the exchequer, resort to extraction of benefits from the recipients of services. This takes the form of cash, gifts, funding personal bills, perquisites, funding admissions, sponsorships etc. The list is exhaustive. The tentacles of C governance spread far and wide and it becomes difficult to pull them out from their strongholds.

Cash is demanded for expediting decisions for favors promised or given. Sometimes promises remain promises even though payments take place. Otherwise service dangles a sword in the form of harassment. So people pay for the service of not harassing. In some cases we find officials accepting cash and gifts amounting to hefty sums for promising the agent or contractor not to harass him, and to overlook delays in the execution of works. These are distinct services rendered by the officials. Perquisites like booking hotel accommodation in five star hotels travel in luxury cars, offer of domestic appliances of all conceivable types, air tickets for travel for family within the country and abroad are examples, which are offshoots of C- governance. These apart, there are novel ways of accepting gratification. These are asking various persons who are the beneficiaries, to sponsor events like admission of children to professional institutions, marriages where each area of activity is assigned to one contractor or agency who will arrange for the supplies but make hush payments in full. Here the ordering official who dispenses the services declares him honest because he says he doesn't touch cash. The beneficiary (recipient) directly makes payments to the institutions and other destinations and thus saves effort, trouble and money foe the official.

Violating norms and rules is no problem for these officials. They will twist facts and rules to their advantage when temptations are heavy and backed by hefty money packs. They don't call it a bribe but service charges. In return for favors received some agents send a blonde (the terminology used is luggage) escort commissioned with the task of providing NLF (night landing facilities). The service seeker will ask the service provider," Sir, do you need any luggage at destination". This is particularly true in the case of many officials who travel a lot.

Harassment is adopted as a technique for extracting cash and other benefits. For this the provider asks for AHF. This means Anti Harassment Fee. This is considered a service and is liberally approved by the entire officialdom covering all hierarchies irrespective of time and place.

These apart, cuts in purchases and commissions take place. The percentages are set prior to finalizing the deal and the manner and form of payment is determined beforehand. There are also conduits (persons) who will mobilize cash and deliver to the provider. The technique used to benefit the beneficiary client is to disqualify the best supplier by declaring his goods as defective. There are inspection agencies that are specially assigned the job. In one case higher price covering kickbacks was offered for supply of aluminum conductors. The seeker got a higher price. When asked how he managed to get it, he said: "we reduce the length of the cable by 250 meters and this covers more than the loss we incur by way of AHF". The receiver honestly inspects the goods without allowing any one else to examine, at delivery site because he knows it is of short length and he alone can certify it as fit and satisfactory.

In appointments C-governance takes place in several forms. Advance payments and part payments are the normal practice. But there are ingenious chaps who come to know about the names of selected candidates. They have close liaison with the personnel department issuing appointment orders. They promise a share of the booty to them also and ask them to withhold the issue of appointment letters for a definite period. During this gap the official visits the various selected candidates, tells them he will get jobs for them. He collects a lump sum amount in advance. The orders are issued. He wins the confidence of the candidates and gets more clients in future. But when he is unable to oblige them he is honest enough to refund the amount in full. This honest deal is given wide publicity, only to bring more victims into his net.

C- Governance eats away resources otherwise available to the community. Costs of projects go up considerably. In construction it is said 20% of the outlay leaks out through this channel of corruption. Inequity is built into the system. Deserving candidates and persons don't get their due for they have not resorted to measures to ensure sure success. The absence of ethics is the cause for this state of affairs. The receiver and giver have jettisoned all value systems and developed an elastic conscience to justify their actions.

Huge purchase, large deals involving millions of dollars bring windfalls to champions of C governance. The collections prior to elections for party funding imply this principle by extending invitations to liberally fill deep pockets for receiving cash.

The funniest thing is that the enforcing agency, whose job is to prevent and detect such types of C-governance official, also falls a victim and benefit by huge inflow of funds and perquisites. There are many in the hierarchy and chain to share the spoils. Examples are many. But with one more we conclude this topic. There are entry points at the borders of states. The vehicles have to produce valid documents for entry. The officials who conduct the checking have an eagle's eye to detect where the client has placed a hefty cover in a designated corner of the shed he is using for official work. In the evening a huge amount accumulates and according to an agreed formula the spoils are shared. Many of them have palatial buildings with all gadgets and amenities, luxury cars and facilities for children to study in the best of professional institutions. All these are the blessings of C- Governance. This is pampered, promoted and perpetuated by the government for all benefit .The only loser and the aggrieved individual is the honest law-aiding citizen. He can only cry for E-governance and Good- governance. But how can he destroy C- governance. Elections at frequent intervals only bring this evil back in greater strength and vigor for all want it badly. We all long for a day when C-government will be wiped out in the interest of sound administration and equity for all citizens.

7. Inviting Business Failure

Business is a productive commercial activity. Its essence is profit. No activity is undertaken by a business organization if it does not yield profits at least in the long run. But there are persons who in their over enthusiasm and entrepreneurial fervor launch and operate the business considering only the investment. They assume returns will accrue. By attending a few management-training programs they pick up some modern management concepts like management by objectives. But when it comes to application they often go by their personal objectives, which clash with those of the company. It is a question of attaining the CEO's objectives, which are different from the company's goals. This is particularly true in the case of small business.

The CEO believes in living an aristocratic life without generating funds. He undertakes extensive travels on the pretext of mobilizing funds and for developing business. But in reality he develops himself not in terms of competence and capability but by increased size of bank balances. He lavishly entertains guests giving them five star lunches, which ultimately makes the organization a cash starved crisis ridden one.

Such a CEO has no patience to do profitability analysis. He assumes profit will accrue and optimistically takes away the fictitious profits even at the commencement of the business, mostly from borrowings or working capital. He gives extensive credit and loans for the mere asking to build business and to earn goodwill. The collateral security is inadequate and often does not provide adequate cover for the loan. In addition, short-term funds are invested in building long-term assets.

The craze for acquisition of machinery blocks available capital. Receivables increase and commission is paid to collect funds. Such commission is often siphoned off by the favorites of the management who have no accountability. The company works without any plan or program. The result is the bottom line shows red.

The management incurs overheads of all kinds to embellish the office. The firm sinks into irreparable loss and liquidation. Here we have an interesting case.

A few promoters in their enthusiasm set up a small bank. They used their contacts and mobilized deposits, which came to a sizeable sum. The top man wanted to give a posh appearance to the office. They took a building on lease and lavishly furnished it. The bank functioned without any plan, budget or program.

Costly chairs, tables, cupboards, locker rooms, and office equipments were bought liberally. The available funds were fully utilized. For advances they again borrowed. Deposits from clients were collected. Again investments took place in ultramodern furniture, computers, stationery and interior decoration. Each official had a cabin and it was lavishly furnished. Air conditioners were installed. Journals and newspapers were subscribed.

Visitors were given a cozy room and furniture to sit and relax. Snacks were served .The staff were paid decent salary, though only for the initial months. Many imaginary posts were advertised to impress the public and to build public image. Even then no one responsible, thought about the main business. They forgot about the need to generate profit. The expenditure always exceeded income. The advances were recklessly given and many of them became sticky. They were not recoverable.

There was heavy investment in unproductive assets. Losses increased and there was no income to pay the salaries. Liquidation was the only alternative and the bank failed. There was a run on the bank and the promoters ran for their lives unable to meet the obligations. That was RJ Bank, which had the unique distinction of going into liquidation because of heavy investment in furniture and office facilities. This cause was highlighted in a report on bank failures. It invited failure and fully succeeded though cheated the depositors.

It is sad to note that even when there is access and availability of expertise and modern management practices, CEOs consciously or otherwise choose the path of ruin. They turn into Cheating and Enjoying Officers. Their optimism pushes them down since it is not backed by competence. Let us hope such cases will be reduced and all business will take advantage of modern knowledge and information for stabilizing the business and thus serve society.

8. Executive Devaluation

Reorganization takes place when functions of departments and executives are reshuffled and realigned to fulfill newly discovered organizational objectives. Executives seek to solve problems by taking right decisions, which for implementation requires strength and support from the relationships between departmental employees in the organization. Successful executive performance requires, inter alia, company environment conducive to morale, emotional stability and incentives to higher levels of performance. Status strengthens the base for establishing such relationships and to make decisions effective. Morale, among other things, involves maintenance of good relations by all employees focusing on a common task. It helps them to work in peace with enthusiasm towards a common goal in a disciplined manner. Factors like inequity, inexplicable differences in remuneration, privileges and perquisites, unnecessary transfers and postings etc. tend to affect the morale of executives. This phenomenon often manifests in developing countries with a less progressive type of management.

Morale is a vital factor in motivation to higher levels of performance. Unless executives are motivated, organizations stand to lose. 'Executive Devaluation' is the lowering of the importance of one executive in relation to the others for reasons illogical and not known to him. It upsets the existing scale of official relationships. These relationships undergo a change and this often affects morale adversely.

Companies and departments reorganize their functions. This results in various types of executive devaluation. A suddenly dawned shallow sense of economy brings abolition of posts causing reversion to some executives with long experience in higher posts. They have to take to post of lower status. Sometimes new posts are created and new hierarchies of personnel arise. The creation of a new level or post at a higher level reduces the importance of the official now immediately below it. Functions are reshuffled. Sometimes duplication of functions takes place or important functions are taken away from the existing incumbent and assigned to one at a lower level without enhancement of the importance of the former's function.

Illogical salary revisions and grant of perquisites affecting a section of executives create disparity compared to those formerly on the same level. Some changes bring high-sounding designations for a few otherwise unimportant posts. Designations like Chief General Manager, Chief Principal Customer Relations Manager are not uncommon even in large organizations. Transfers and postings bring functions not related to the basic skills of the executive There also arises great distance in communicating between the levels in the organization. All these result in a particular executive being referred to as a figurehead. Thus the process of 'devaluation' takes place.

Executive devaluation cannot be ascribed to any single cause. Broadly it is the result of expediency, absence of well-defined basic functions, organizational relationships and faulty policy regarding recruitment, promotion, transfers, and postings. Unimpressive designations to executives of high responsibility place them in a position of not gaining recognition and attention sometimes from within the organization and often from the public.

It often happens that the brand image attached to a designation determines one's status in the eyes of the employees and the public. A junior official is appointed to a post, which traditionally and in the interest of efficiency was held by a senior, experienced, and competent official. The reverse also happens. A man of rich and diversified experience is placed in charge of an insignificant post. Inadequate appraisal of operational needs, absence of job specifications, inadequate understanding of staff and line functions, determining organizational pattern to fit in with personalities and their abilities, incorrect performance appraisal, lack of objectivity and neglect of functional needs also give rise to this feature. There may not be any definite idea of organizational needs for longer period or for different stages of growth of the organization or a department.

Devaluation can result in serious consequences. Apart from reduction in salary and or status for the concerned officials, it may give rise to paper tigers and friction between 'devalued executives' and new bosses. Since status is distorted command becomes difficult. It may breed indifference among the 'devalued' executives. The result can be low efficiency and sometimes the flight of talented men.

To avoid or at least to minimize such ill effects, organizations may do well to bear in mind the following considerations while reorganizing their functions. The objective of maintaining morale at all levels should be kept in mind throughout the process of reorganization and particularly during implementation. Before work on reorganization commences, the employees should be informed of the reasons for such a step. Executives whose positions are abolished should be given equally important assignments without reduction in their salaries and perquisites. When news posts are created or appointments made, it will be helpful to keep in mind the demands of the organization for a long period, say five years to permit the executive to remain in the same position and to contribute more efficiency. There should be minimum changes in designations to give effect to the transfer of basic functions only.

An organization chart clearly demarcating the levels and the line of command will help to clarify the position of executives. Salary should considerably reflect the nature of responsibility to be held and systematic review of job requirements will ensure equity. The impact of reorganization on the morale of various categories of staff should be considered. Those responsible for reorganization have to ensure that as rule additions and changes take place within the framework originally planned for the organization. The organization should have a personnel policy that flows from its objectives. The policy should be made known to all employees at the time of joining the organization.

Status is the respect commanded by virtue of one's position in the organization. While the individual executive has to build up status by his ability and handling of situations, the base has to be provided by the organization. If reorganization brings no significant downward shit in the base, there is no danger of executive devaluation.

9. Managing Greed

Men want to satisfy their wants. Economics deals with wants satisfaction. Wants and desires multiply They are the indiscriminate offspring of the mind .When they are satisfied at the lowest level more and more desires and wants manifest and demand fulfillment. This becomes greed. The nature of greed and its growth are like pouring ghee into fire. The intensity becomes great. When resources are not available to satisfy greed, crooked methods are sought. Greed commands resources and this need not be based on priority. So resources are cornered by people who perpetuate and promote greed. Though we may call many of them entrepreneurs, many turn out to be thieves of society.

When the tendency to satisfy greed becomes predominant in society such a society adopts all means fair and foul to muster resources. This leads to extensive borrowing since own resources may be inadequate. Excessive borrowing creates a situation that repayment of loans becomes difficult and default occurs. This sets in motion a chain reaction and the economy collapses causing fall in employment and rise in economic misery. The lone culprit is greed.

Thus the bane of society is greed and if we want to improve society and its economic condition we must curb greed. Greed results in wastage of resources. The recent stock market crash and global meltdown confirm this phenomenon.

Recent global melt down had its origin in human greed which prompted individuals to acquire assets even at the risk of heavy borrowing. Banks welcomed borrowers to further their business. This led to business boom and later a bubble burst. We are yet to recover from the onslaught of this big hit. Share markets crashed. Banks collapsed .This resulted in loss of millions of jobs. Loss of income caused proliferation of misery. Economic theory based on multiplicity of desires and wants can only offer a faulty structure with loose foundation.

How long it will last is any body's guess. How far can the wants theory of progress go?

Are not resources cornered and wasted?

Are there not priorities for human existence? Why not upgrade human values which will definitely scale down greed and ensure better standards of living for all instead of extreme happiness for a few and acute misery for many. Controlling greed is the function of controlling the mind with the power of the intellect. If our educational system can achieve this in a decade steadily we will definitely march towards stable progress without tears. Let us start building up a global value system relinquishing greed. Let us not salute greed as an engine of economic progress

10. New Breed of CEOs

Corporate greed has manifested in different corners of the globe. Big companies make galloping progress in growth, sales and profits. They imbibe and propagate the concept of business as a noble profession. They introduce healthy management practices. However, such nobility exists only when ethics becomes an integral part of such a business philosophy. CEOs with high degree of ethics and competence are a great asset to organizations and society. They create wealth and ensure sustainability of the enterprise which they built. They are really Chief Executive Officers.

These days business without ethics earns respectability in society. Really speaking, it is business built on loot. This philosophy of business loot, unfortunately, is gaining ground and popularity. That is why we have booming business followed by catastrophic collapse.

Greed manifests when ethics doesn't support human desires. The result is crash, collapse and calamity. World economy is reeling under this economic malady. The thrust for such economic calamity starts with recession and is given by CEOs.

When CEOs become Chief Embezzlement Officers the downturn takes place in organizations. Greed and irresponsibility dominate and downfall of organizations and economy with series of chain reactions takes place. We have examples of Enron, Satyam with their contemporaries and counterparts worldwide who brought about collapse of several banks and institutions.

Efforts are made to recover reversing the trend towards economic disaster.

For this first recovery of the backbones of CEOs has to be effected. This is not easy unless they learn from mistakes and take care not to repeat them. No amount of money pumped into the system will bring relief and recovery unless their managerial backbone with ethical content is recovered fully.

These CEOs belong to a new breed and they replace execution with embezzlement. Personal aggrandizement becomes the motto and thus society suffers through massive unemployment. Fake documents, diversion of funds for personal objectives, atrocious audit practices, laxity in government control, are all responsible for this phenomenon of galloping greed and irresponsibility where the reins are lost and disaster strikes. If this is not to happen in future, along with scientific progress, management techniques, wisdom should be recognized and elevated to a high pedestal.

Wisdom recognizes ethics and values and is rooted in the sustainability principle which is also applicable to the concept of growth and economy. Greed should be checked. It is here the great eastern philosophy becomes relevant, important and practical.

Wealth should be accumulated only subject to righteousness. The same is the case with human desires. This simple formula is forgotten in the thick of the smoke caused by greed and craving for corporate growth by any means.

In the interest of posterity now at least, let all business schools and institutions concerned with the economic development take a pledge that they will evolve a kind of knowledge that will be practical and at the same time rooted in ethics and righteousness. They should turn out stuff that will turn into real CEOs who undertake great tasks of execution and not CEOs who are Chief Embezzlement Officers. Then only we can have a stable, happy and sustainable world.

11. Consumerism & Market Crash

Decades ago the famous economist and Nobel Laureate Jan Tin Bergen observed:

"Generally the rich of the earth should prepare for themselves for a simpler life in the future. The leading philosophy of the present, which always asks for more material goods and does not attach many values at simplicity of life or modesty in claims, has to be replaced by alternative philosophies, and surely much could be learnt from Mahatma Gandhi's words and example. The real values of life do contain a sufficient quantity of food and shelter; but it is not necessary to have the luxuries now aimed at. Cultural values will have to be 'upgraded' again. The tremendous waste on armament and outer space research should be curtailed".

Let us see the relevance of these golden words of the great economist in the context of the global financial crisis we are witnessing. The world is shaken to the bones by the tidal wave of economic disaster starting with the collapse of the US stock market. Many large banking companies are forced into liquidation as if they were victims of an atomic blast. The resulting loss to institutions and individuals is colossal .Its tentacles of damage are spreading far and wide to other countries and economies. Share values have collapsed.

The losses are in billions of dollars. Some large financial companies wound up. Many others are in the path of closure taking their turn. A few shocked and frustrated individuals unable to bear the loss commit suicide. At least in one case one family was completely eliminated. The family a few seconds ago worth $50 million is worth nothing now.

Several countries find themselves in the hit list of the disaster wave. Many lose jobs for companies are forced to retrench and close down. There are no takers for the assets offered for sale. The liquidity crisis is severe. The US Government pumped in $700 billion to salvage the economy. The impact and the beneficial results are yet to emerge. We hope for the best.

Economists may break their heads to find the cause of this great economic malady... But common sense encased in wisdom tells us that the entire disease has originated from human greed. This is attested by the words of the Nobel Laureate. Jan Tin Bergen. Is it not greed fanned by consumerism which is worshipped, promoted and taken as an index of progress? More and more possessions and the quest for higher standards of living have taken us to this plight. Is it the hall mark of growth? Are we not in the trap of desires fanned by conspicuous consumption? Is it not the outcome of growing expectations which turn into cravings and greed?

Should we not salute our ancient wisdom in the matter of wealth acquisition and creation? If only we adhere to it we would have earned wealth subject to righteousness and eliminated greed substantially from the economic system. The economy would have been value driven and not greed driven. We would have respected the principle of sustainability in all areas of human activity and ensured life balance.

When we ignored these fundamentals our reins were broken and economic depression sets in with snowballing effect. Expectations are a function of the mind. They grow and transform into greed when intellect loses its power of discrimination. Risks go out of hand and calculations go astray. Can we not become bold without being rash? Can we not restrain ourselves from entering uncertain crocodile infested waters? When uncertainty and greed dominate market crash becomes inevitable. It is only a question of time.

The magnitude of loss is not yet determined and known. We keep our fingers crossed

Should we not save posterity from such economic disasters? If we want to make a beginning in this direction everyone will do well to chain the demon of galloping greed from causing global havoc and misery.

II. Corrective Action

1. Ancient Wisdom

This section deals with a vital area, which has been perhaps left out by the management consultancy profession. This could bring substantial benefits to organizations and ultimately to humanity in terms of wealth, happiness and sustainability of resources. Being a noble profession, management consultancy welcomes knowledge from all disciplines and areas of knowledge for solution of managerial problems. It has benefited considerably by opening its doors to welcome knowledge from many areas. It has contributed to the enrichment of the management profession by formulating approaches having wide applications.

However, it is sad to note that the most promising source of strength for the profession to benefit organizations and humanity has not been given adequate importance. The purpose of this series of articles is to bring out the quintessence of the knowledge, -vital for value creation, innovation and knowledge management.

Value creation is creating value by applying knowledge available to us in any area of human activity with a management orientation. This is to bring about productive and useful results in organizations benefiting several people. . Innovation is bringing out something new but which can revolutionize our ways of living. Knowledge management is managing or making use of available knowledge for attaining definite objectives. Management consultancy has the objective of designing and applying concepts, tools and techniques for the improved performance of organizations. This has to be consistent with ethics and resource availability.

Let us consider for a while what is happening to value creation? Here it is worthwhile raising a few questions. Are we creating value always to attain the maximum potential? In terms of monetary and production value we are adding to value. But in terms of consumer satisfaction, happiness and sustainability of resources are we adding value? Are we not producing low priority goods and services on the pretext of economic growth? Tacit consent is given to unethical ways of facing competition and making profits.

In reality there is knowledge explosion but not always in the right direction. We all ideally aim that this knowledge should benefit a vast majority of people. Knowledge is not required for knowledge sake. It should be sustainable knowledge. It should be such that its growth has to be only to the extent ethics support it. Otherwise that knowledge becomes harmful or redundant.

In effect a small section of people benefit substantially and the others get marginal benefit. It is this distorted knowledge management that restricts the field of operations of management consultancy confining it to industry and organizations.

We talk about systems approach for solving problems. This envisages a total approach to problem solving using relevant knowledge from all disciplines considering the system and subsystems. But have we seriously tried to use relevant valuable knowledge from spirituality-based sources, which constitute a subsystem of knowledge? These sources originate from ancient scriptures of wisdom, which greatly emphasize human excellence. They focus on the individual. We know human resources are very important. We all appreciate the role of motivation in achieving performance. But do we recognize the power within man to excel in performance and how this could be tapped and realized in terms of potential. This is an omission needing immediate attention and correction.

This vital knowledge is available to us for thousands of years. Great sages of vision, who had only the good of humanity in mind, evolved this. There is very little evidence of the quintessence of our ancient wisdom being used by the management consultancy profession in an organized manner.

It is the spirit within man, which makes living possible and in whose presence alone all human action and achievement are possible. It is the divinity that really illumines the functioning of the body. It imparts strength to men and managers if they realize its presence and are attached to it. The thought that one is the spirit gives strength and this is a vital force, which motivates. It helps to view the body as an instrument of action. It propels one to excel in performance without craving for rewards.

The inspiration one gets from such a faith is tremendous. This created many leaders in India and abroad. They shook the world with their power of thoughts and actions. Such men had a conceptual approach not confined to any organization but to the whole country and even beyond. It is this approach that gave them a vision and dynamism to achieve human excellence. They were real leaders worthy of emulation.

Systems Approach

Mahatma Gandhi was an example. He conceived India as one integrated whole. He was highly motivated. He had a supra ordinary goal. He lived and worked with a sense of fulfillment without expecting anything except the welfare of his countrymen. If management consultancy imparts this strength to leadership development we will have an increasing number of highly productive and motivated leaders. This will occur not only in industrial and business organizations but in other fields of national importance also. Their contribution will be undoubtedly positive, productive and far-reaching. Same is the case with managers and entrepreneurs. They will be charged with the power of dynamism to make their contribution more effective and substantial.

Scriptures and Wisdom

The insights into our ancient scriptures reveal genuine wisdom, which if applied will definitely help the profession to be more effective. The offshoots of such a value creating philosophy will be of a high order. Such a list will cover time management, motivation, functional specialization, human relations, conflict elimination, ethics oriented strategy, energy conservation, cost reduction, waste elimination, human excellence etc. The philosophy definitely adds to value. It ensures better knowledge management.

The conceptual skills are embedded in works of ancient wisdom. We apply them to the enterprise and that skill becomes important for the CEO. With a universal mind the perspective of the CEO changes. He broadens his vision and is able to ensure and discharge his social responsibilities, which are cared for spontaneously. There will be a natural built in mechanism for resolving conflicts in organizations because the degree of understanding will be great.

Let us consider some areas where the ancient wisdom rooted in spirituality is of help to us. It clearly emphasizes the importance of goal setting for the individual.

Management also stresses this whether it is an organization or a department. Individual goals crystallized will be tuned to the organization's goal and management by objectives will be better realized. The merit here is something unique in that such objectives and actions are based on ethics.

Management training is considered an important aspect of executive and organization development. This is preparing the executive for higher responsibilities. Ancient wisdom does this in a more effective way. It lays down discipline-Spartan discipline, through techniques like yoga to tune the body and health, and meditation to tune the mind for concentration. It stresses the role of positive thinking for purifying thoughts facilitating right decisions and judgment. It creates leadership models.

The kings and leaders of the past were role models and they set examples of good administration. Case studies for leadership development, duties and responsibilities and interpersonal relations, from the great epics like Ramayana and Mahabharata help to improve leadership training.

Management lays stress on training, which is equipping oneself for executive position. Ancient wisdom emphasizes equipping oneself with qualities for learning and grasping. It stipulated proper diets and physical exercise for men of action to withstand strain. Yoga is considered to be a very effective technique. It is effectively equipping oneself unlike the holiday approach of the modern executive. We applaud modern expressions like executive lunch but fail to understand the prevalence of better diet packages for men thousands of years ago.

The conceptual skills are embedded in works of ancient wisdom. We apply them to the enterprise and that skill becomes important for the CEO. When one develops a universal mind the perspective of the CEO changes. He broadens his vision and is able to ensure and discharge his social responsibilities, which are cared for spontaneously. There will be a natural built in mechanism for resolving conflicts in organizations because the degree of understanding will be great.

Let us consider some areas where the ancient wisdom rooted in spirituality is of help to us. It clearly emphasizes the importance of goal setting for the individual. Management also stresses this whether it is an organization or a department. Individual goals crystallized will be tuned to the organization's goal and management by objectives will be better realized. The merit here is something unique in that such objectives and actions are based on ethics.

Management training is considered an important aspect of executive and organization development. This is preparing the executive for higher responsibilities. Ancient wisdom does this in a more effective way. It lays down discipline-

Spartan discipline, through techniques like yoga to tune the body and health, and meditation to tune the mind for concentration. It stresses the role of positive thinking for purifying thoughts facilitating right decisions and judgment. It creates leadership models.

Self Management

The management consultancy profession should focus on cooperation than competition. The former avoids waste and saves resources whereas the latter promotes waste and boosts up costs. Globally this principle of cooperation in lieu of competition has been accepted. That is why we have organizations like the WTO, EEC to ensure smooth economic transactions between countries.

It is beneficial to focus on self-management to promote human excellence, which is one of the most important objectives of management consultancy. The focus on training the body, mind and intellect for maintaining health, fitness, discipline, stress free existence and clear thinking for right decisions is ensured.

In all areas of consultancy the basic anchor should be righteousness. Wealth creation and acquisition should be based on this principle. This will remove greed and corrupt tendencies in organizations. It is beneficial to include among objectives of organizations the following important one- to create wealth subject to the condition that such process is firmly rooted in righteousness. The same approach is applicable to satisfying consumer desires. The availability of harmful goods and services should be restricted and gradually withdrawn.

Management consultancy is a noble profession. It can act as a catalyst to effect significant changes in standards of living and economic progress with sustainability. It should give emphasis on creating wealth in sectors where the poor people will largely benefit so that poverty will be eliminated over a period of time. All actions should be based on righteousness, i.e., fairness and transparency in dealings. Training programs should offer this as the thrust area. If this fundamental aspect is ignored the economic system will operate to the common detriment. The activities of the organization and society should be value driven and not greed driven.

This may appear to be a utopian philosophy of management. But we have to aim high and keep the ideal up and not pull it down in the name of practicality. If we do so then we are elevating the status of a thief to that of an effective, efficient and most successful manager. This is because he does not use any resources of his own to attain his objectives of stealing. Even the tools he uses are stolen. The access to concepts and methods for human excellence implied and advocated in the works of ancient wisdom confers several benefits on consultants. The Bhagavad-Gita gives us all essential knowledge for human excellence. It ensures sustainability in several areas like environment, resources exploitation, technology etc. At the individual level whether it is employee or CEO it can definitely bring results. These could be in terms of conservation of energy, resources, industrial peace, and balanced infrastructure and overall growth of the economy. Such growth will ensure equity, fairness and life balance.

Any individual who is trained with armor of spirituality will be an asset to society. He will not steal. Nor will he create law and order problems. He will enjoy life and make others happy. He will let others live happily. This is true whether he is a CEO or employee or a citizen. It is hoped the future generations of management consultants will seriously dive deep to the springs of ancient wisdom. It is our prayer that they draw as much as possible, modify and perfect them. It is our fervent hope that they will graft them into the consultancy profession so that organizations and societies benefit substantially.

.2. Enrich Management

Management is the art of attaining definite objectives often with inadequate resources. Mankind owes so much to Bhagavad-Gita for its teachings many of which have management implications particularly in the area of human resources development. The economy of a nation is the karma (action) of its business leaders. There is nothing higher than the Gita as a source of motivation and excellence for nation building and leadership development. The economic future of any country rests on the young managers of today. Only men of character and vision deeply rooted in management and spiritual strength can make a nation culturally and economically strong. This should be the goal and message of modern management.

Many managers feel rudderless for want of a proper value system. Pressure groups gain ascendancy in organizations and in society. They displace sanity, reason and love and install corruption, incompetence and greed in their place. We have come across several cases in support of this phenomenon. In pursuit of wealth they neglect their own duty to society. Violence and frustration, give rise to constant mental conflict and intellect is clouded. Agitations and strikes plague society and work havoc causing huge erosion of resources. The result is substandard performance in all areas of activity and wastage of resources. This is exactly what management and wisdom seek to avoid.

The rudderless performance is the result of imbalance in the body, mind and intellect system. Expectations grow fast and are not fulfilled. The enormous intangible resource within man is not tapped and its potential not realized. This reservoir of talent and energy is mostly wasted. . In short we are not managing our God given internal resources effectively and for the benefit of society.

What is the remedy? Management. Yes, Management that will rely on ancient Indian wisdom, which is the world's precious and priceless heritage. It emphasizes the need for mind control, positive thinking and a healthy body.

Here comes the role of self-management. Spirituality provides insight into the knowledge of "knowledge". Management is the noblest of noble professions. Both are creative. Both stress on optimum resource utilization. Our objective should be to excel in a chosen field for activity. All of us want happiness, which is a state of mind. It does not mean the joy of possessing material objects. It is attaining peace of mind and remaining in that state without any break. In that state of mind great contributions to society take place. The examples of great leaders reveal their strength derived from the inspiration sprouting from the bottom of the reservoir of wisdom evolved from spiritual strength.

What should we do? The concept of empathy widely discussed in management can be extended to include respect for all. It is respecting the human side of enterprise. It is enlarging the scope of the Y theory of Mc Gregor, an authority on human relations. We must learn to love all creations in the universe. Our environmentalists discovered the need for conservation of natural wealth only recently whereas Indian sages (Rishis) discovered and propagated this concept thousands of years ago. We must stretch our minds to the farthest limit. The mind is a $10 billion gift. Here the concept of developing a universal mind becomes relevant. It is an extension of the management concept of thinking big. It is the highest development of the concept of conceptual skill. Conserving our energy and cultivating positive values will greatly help the cause of management. We must seek and master the true knowledge, the knowledge of all knowledge, and the light of all lights. This is royal wisdom. It is the purifier, wh.ch will help to liquidate all evil tendencies in the mind. There will be no source of disturbance and one can attain total freedom from stress, which is a curse of the modern executive. It enables one to discharge all obligatory duties faithfully. One's intellect will be calm and peace sets in. One will not entertain any greed prompted thought.

Take care of the body through yoga, *pranayama* and control of food. Yoga asana with proper breathing will ensure stamina, efficiency and good health. By living in the present one can manage time better and make it more productive. This concept of time management is deeply imbedded in ancient Indian wisdom. One will be free from preoccupations. One will not regret about the mistakes of the past or have anxieties about the future. One can aim at excellence cherishing age-old time-tested values. Spiritual strength is the greatest asset. A manager benefits considerably by developing and holding on to it. It helps to develop muscles of iron and nerves of steel.

It is worth remembering the old saying "Better a moment of glow than a lifetime of smoke". Thus we achieve a better quality of life and TQM.This should be the message to young managers. Modern management will gain a lot if it brings spirituality in its fold as part of a systems approach to efficient value based management

3. Gold Mine

Of all faculties of man, the mind is a remarkable one, a 10 billion dollar gift. It is said that if a machine is to be made to discharge the functions of the mind, it will cost at least $10 billion. Even then it will be a poor substitute for the mind, which travels faster than light. The moment you desire to be in a distant 5 billion light years away your mind takes you there. When we are blessed with such a precious gift, we have to ask ourselves whether we making the best use of it for the benefit of society and us. The answer is 'No'.

The mind is a flow of thoughts occurring at random and sometimes with a purpose. It entertains negative and positive thoughts on different occasions. It has great potential for doing good and bad. Sometimes it is dull and at other times it is very active. It is restless and this aggravates if neglected. There is a case of a monkey to illustrate the seriousness of the restless mind. The monkey by itself is restless. It got intoxicated with liquor. In that condition a scorpion stung it. On the way it was seized by a devil. Now you can imagine its condition as a result of the cumulative impact of all these influences. So is the case with the human mind, which is uncared and nurtured with thoughts of anger and greed. We have sense organs for hearing, seeing, tasting, touching and smelling. Without the mind these organs are only matter. It is the mind behind the organs that makes them functional.

The choice of thoughts is decided by the intellect, which weighs pros and cons, discriminates and decides. The seeds of wars are sown in the minds of men. This shows its destructive nature. The seeds of good deeds also originate in the mind and they form one's character and ultimately destiny. We have seen great scientists and leaders who applied their minds positively upholding noble and lofty ideals, ultimately bringing about great inventions, discoveries and achievements. We are not really attaining the potential of the mind. Except in rare cases, Hardly 0.1 per cent of it is utilized Human beings who have achieved high are those who have tapped the reservoir of energy within. Others fritter away such energy in ephemeral pleasures, entertainments, time wasting occupations, nonsensical conversation and gossip, which benefit none. The mind is a double-edged sword that can be use for killing an enemy or save a person. The great achievements of Nobel laureates reveal the positive and fruitful use of mind whereas those using destructive means reveal negative applications. Great men control the mind, conserve energy to benefit society and get a sense of fulfillment. They develop powers of concentration. Meditation helps to control the mind by focusing on a single idea or object on which thought flows without any break.

Intelligent men believe in living in the present. It is worth realizing that the present alone is within our control. The past is gone. We have no control over it. Today's present becomes tomorrow's past. Today's future becomes tomorrow present. So there is no past or future but only present. We must productively use the present moment before us and live in the present to get the best results from our efforts. We should not have preoccupations. . It does not mean we should not think of the future or learn from the past. We can learn lessons from the past to make improvements in the present, which will have impact on the future. We can plan for the future to devote our time usefully. Future is shaped by what we do in the present.

Desire originates in mind. If allowed to go unchecked it multiplies and creates agitations dissipating energy. If desires are not fulfilled anger arises and mental agitation follows. A satisfied desire leads to craving and soon greed overtakes us. All these depict the unbridled condition of the mind resulting in mental ill health and unhappiness. So we have to keep the mind steady and calm.

There is a beautiful example given in the Hindu scriptures, which makes us understand the role of the mind. The human body is compared to a chariot. The five senses are the horses and the reins represent the mind. The charioteer is the intellect. The occupant is God who is the witness to everything. For excellence in performance the senses have to be controlled. The mind does this under proper control and direction. For effective functioning it has to take orders from the intellect, which directs it without allowing going astray. When this happens harmoniously the chariot goes smoothly along the right royal road and to the destination.

It is important for all and particularly for business executives to keep the mind steady and calm. Executives suffer stress, which is an undesirable experience. Everyone wants relief from stress. It clouds ones thinking, saps energy and health. The result is that a stress-affected person explodes out of bad temper. Some executives howl like wild beasts at subordinates and believe in the practice of animal control. This sets in motion a chain reaction and strained relationships in the organization. Progressive organizations will do well to include meditation as part of management techniques to attain human excellence and organizational harmony. They can control executive behavior molding it for organizational effectiveness. Laughter relaxes the mind and is the best medicine to relief stress. It costs nothing. Just like air, space, water, fire and earth it is free. The mind becomes fresh. Laugher tones up the system. Laughter therapy has come to be accepted as a useful technique for attaining mental health and harmony. Let us realize and fully utilize the great gift God has bestowed on us. Great achievers in any field are those who realized this potential and developed a universal mind. Let us move in that direction and inspire posterity. Thus we build a better world to live and enjoy.

4. Knowledge with Spiritual Content

In the Twenty-first century we have achieved amazing progress materially in raising the standard of living of the people in general. There has been tremendous knowledge explosion and the knowledge industry is growing rapidly. The world has shrunk in terms of distances and become a village with vast connectivity thanks to the Internet and jet travel. Science and technology are advancing at tremendous speed. There is increase in GDP of most countries. Medical science has advanced and longevity of man has increased. More countries are joining the list of developed countries. Opportunities for material advancement are increasing.

Have we attained the quality of life warranted by the rate and quantum of progress we have achieved? The ingredients of this are good health, positive thinking, improvement in character; compassion for others; inherent tendency and urge to help others, capacity to do one's allotted duty in the most efficient manner, maintaining a sustainable environment etc.

We are unable to make full use of the knowledge that is generated. This also raises the question whether what we acquire is relevant knowledge to improve our quality of life or harmful knowledge that adversely affects the quality of life.

Crimes of various types are on the increase. Values, which maintained the relationships in society, are declining and disappearing. We have so many specialized courses and programs of education. But they seek to improve the material advancement of man. They provide career opportunities. But they draw blank when coming to character formation, which is a major indication of man's real progress and quality of life. Have we made any progress in improving the character of man? This task is left to religious and spiritual organizations. Is not character formation an ingredient of economic development?

Progress can be sustained only if any program implemented is rooted in human character. This means a well disciplined code of conduct self imposed by the individual for the best contribution from him and for the good of society.

The ingredients of quality of life are: pollution free environment, harmonious relations within communities, decline in crime, value based leadership, a feeling of safety, absence of fear, positive roles for government, institutions, citizens, maintenance of law and order, sifting relevant knowledge and rejecting irrelevant knowledge, absence of discrimination among people positive role of media, press, films, books and substituting the philosophy of glorification of crime and immorality by that of glorification of character, contribution and social harmony.

There is dethronement of wisdom. The great and cherished treasured values are thrown to the winds by a vast majority of the population who live a life at the level of the senses. Are we making any serious effort to reverse the trend except crying from roof tops that the scourge of terrorism and vice afflicts the world? Is it not time to wake up and act? We realize that cancer caused by tobacco use or smoking is an evil and treatment of this disease costs more than the revenue earned from tobacco products. Why not we realize that lack of character in humans is the chronic disease.

To reverse the trend and reduce the intensity of the damage caused why not give priority to character formation and development in all our learning and research methodologies? Why not incorporate this as an essential ingredient of progress in all branches of knowledge. There is no dearth of resources for reversing the adverse trend. Words of ancient wisdom are contained in the scriptures of all religions. We have to dig out and use them liberally. The curative properties of these works are great and marvelous and have been proved by the test of time.

Texts like the Bhagavad-Gita contain enormous potential for the benefit of mankind. It focuses only on the positive aspects and the good of man. It is a tool of motivation and human excellence. It has relevance to nation building and character and leadership development. Only men of character and vision in any field of activity, be it science, economics or politics, alone can deliver the goods on a lasting basis and ensure global prosperity and harmony. They will be anchored in spirituality. Only then we will have real progress with global harmony and happiness.

The human mind has to set its direction towards achieving this goal. It does not matter if it takes time. But the progress achieved will be lasting and solid. Otherwise we will produce more and more Nobel laureates but also a cluster of sick societies where man is preoccupied only with selfish interests, leaving the poor to their fate from which relief is almost impossible for them for decades.

This calls for the best of management of the human faculties at the individual level. It is self-management. It means rectifying the imbalance in the body, mind and intellect function. It will richly draw on the reservoir of talent and energy from inside, the God given internal resources, effectively for the benefit of society. Wisdom cannot be told. It has to be acquired through reflections on experience. This has to be done through mind control, positive thinking, and a healthy body.

We must stretch our minds to the farthest limit; take care of the body through yogic exercises, proper breathing and control of food. Yoga postures with proper breathing will ensure stamina, efficiency and good health. By living in the present we can manage time better. We can attain excellence by adding to our work age-old time-tested values. Spiritual strength that comes from the faith in a supreme power above man is the greatest asset. Man benefits by developing and holding on to it. We gain considerably if every field of human activity brings value systems in its fold.

Management is the art of attaining definite objectives often with inadequate resources. Every organization uses resources to meet needs, which are formulated in the form of objectives. These resources have to be used

5. Time a Prime Resource

Time is the measurement of interval between two events or experiences. Unlike other factors it is a fixed one. If not rightly used for thought or action it is a waste, never to be recovered. An executive has always to think of action. The relevant experiences before such an action have an effect on the nature of action taken during such an interval.

Similarly the experience during the time under consideration definitely leaves a result depending on the soundness of action taken during that period. So to ensure that subsequent periods bring desirable, tangible and beneficial results, like any other resource, time available should be intelligently utilized.

Time is non-recoverable and hence a critical resource. The other resources are men, materials, machines and money. These resources in different combinations, within a time span, produce results. They are achieved with reference to definite needs, which have been identified. So a business executive has to match the needs and resources in relation to the time available for achieving definite results. If such time is not available he will have to use more of other resources within the available time.

Time and action

An executive takes decisions triggering actions to achieve pre-determined results. Action leads to consequences, which reflect also the forces of the environment. Speedy decisions bring quicker actions and results. Whether the decision is right or wrong depends on the soundness of the process up to the decision making level. These processes in turn depend on the marshalling of facts relevant to the decision before the time of action.

Organization

For a business executive action has to be always in terms of results to be achieved as stated by the management through clear objectives. The time available to him, apart from that for his personal and family needs, should be solely used for the growth of his organization. Such time will also include time needed for self-improvement and proficiency in job. His thoughts can directly be canalized towards his managerial functions. Once the planning stage is over he acts mostly through the team working with him

While discharging his official duties he should always remember these relationships in the organization, the functions directly under his charge and the main objectives of the organization. Within a given time he can achieve results. This depends upon his mental and intellectual equipment and how he acts or makes use of his available time. While this is what one normally expects from an executive, let us consider what actually happens in reality. There are several instances where executives work in a leisurely manner. There may be too many men, which often causes clash of priorities. In addition constraints of environment and procedures consume most of the available time. Absence of a system necessitates consideration of a matter in a repetitive time consuming way of trial and error. Executives find time hanging on them and the absence of a creative outlook towards life and work causes boredom.

Inadequate communication facilities or lack of supplies consume much time adversely affecting results. A loose organization results in wastage of time on knowing who is doing what, who has authority to do, and who the person to be contacted etc is. Even with all these the absence of a clear goal dissipates the efforts of the staff. There is no sense of urgency; no order of priority and absence of constant review with the result the time element in producing results is forgotten.

These factors mainly arise due to lack of clear objectives. If not all departments will function efficiently considering the time availability and work schedule. There are other contributory factors. These are ignorance of employees about the value of time, incompetence, and absence of essential facilities, indiscipline, and presence of square pegs in round holes and the lack of recognition for good ideas.

Further an executive's time is wasted if he is regularly used for a job, which could be done by another on lower salary. This practice of exploiting an executive's presence to do an absentee's work, irrespective of job content, is a poor method of using his time.

Excuses

Square pegs in round holes may refuse to be convinced and give excuses for not getting things done. One important point for executives to remember is that some employees exploit the facility of free access to their bosses. Forgetting the value of time for the bosses, they introduce in the conversation questions, seeking details like color, shape and weight of tomatoes in South American countries and how vegetable cutlets are prepared in Antarctica.

This may be a source of adding to their general knowledge. But imagine how much time is axed by such questions particularly when answered. If the boss ventures to tolerate this, the disease will spread and contaminate others. If the proportion of such personnel increases in the organization, the executive with a creative mind will find his creativity choked. Thus *worklessness* is an enemy of efficiency. It makes serious inroads into the precious time of those who value their time. *Solution*

Now let us consider the solution to the problem of time squeeze, though it can be only a partial remedy. The prime need of the executive should be to regard time as a resource. In fact it should be given the importance of a critical resource in management since it is more precious than any other resource. Once lost it can never be recovered or substituted. He can effectively manage time over which he has full control provided he knows how to manage its use. For this he should obtain essential facilities particularly for communication. The management should recognize the need for such facilities and offer them voluntarily and ungrudgingly rather than waiting to give them after repeated demands and bargaining.

The objectives of the executive should be:
1. To save time by releasing time from unproductive and less important activities and
2. To get the maximum results per period.
It is useful to examine how these objectives could be achieved. Faster movement, speedy decisions and removing constrains in work help to save time.

Simple procedure

The executive should ensure means of faster communication, clear and simpler procedures and minimum inter personal and departmental consultation. He should minimize constrains and introduce system into his official and personal life so that decisions are made as a routine activity, releasing time for more important and complex work. He should have a clear and definite goal and all other sub goals directed towards it.

He should canalize his efforts and those of his subordinates in furthering the main goal and constantly improve his competence to excel in his job. Through self-improvement and developing subordinates he will have more time for creative and productive work.

For realizing most out of each minute he should plan ahead the needs, use of resources and the use of time. Thus at the time of action he can double his output.

Solution

The executive should organize his efforts to adhere to the schedule. It is necessary for him to be up-to-date with information relevant to his field of work. This enables him to save time, which otherwise is spent in hunting for the material at the last minute. Above all he should work out the most efficient way of getting a job done. He should identify deviations from standards, analyze them and minimize the time for corrective action. Management should give him authority to command necessary resources.

An executive by his own efforts cannot achieve the best results from the use of his time, although he forms part of the management. The organization has to be molded to achieve such a purpose. The company has to provide executives all facilities essential to achieve the goal of the organization. Only then managers can manage time effectively and productively.

6. Impart Spiritual Strength

In the pursuit of economic progress and higher standards of living nations often lose sight of the quality of life of citizens. There are various quality of life indices like the state of education, health, housing infrastructure etc. However, wide inequalities in income and privileges exist resulting in strife and squalor. Though the human being is recognized as an important resource, human excellence is rarely achieved except in fits and starts.

The lack of a concerted institutional approach by organizations to attain human excellence, focusing on the individual, brings about a cumulative impact pulling down the quality of life, though other quality of life indices show a positive trend. Pockets of poverty alongside oases of wealth still exist. It is here spirituality comes to our rescue imparting strength to economics and management with lasting beneficial results.

Absence of spiritual content manifests through lack of positive value systems in economic planning, business and management. The adverse effect of this omission is reflected in massive corruption, criminality, frauds, embezzlement, unhealthy personnel policies, cheating, leakages and wastages in the economy. There are also unethical practices like profiteering based on greed and dilution of quality of products and services. Often even the most competent professional who has potential to contribute to enhance the quality of life succumbs to temptations. This damages the reputation of the product and the organization he serves. Why does this happen?

Management which welcomes knowledge from all disciplines rarely seeks and applies knowledge from spiritual sources. Many consider such knowledge as inconclusive and non verifiable in terms of results. This is a fallacy. There has been no determined effort to give a fair trial to the spiritual content of the knowledge and its application to economics and management.

We manage all resources through man. The organs of action together with the faculties of mind and intellect constitute the human resource. Very little is done to manage effectively the tangible and intangible resources within man.

When we buy a home appliance or gadget we are supplied with a booklet of instructions to guide us to use it for getting the best results. Without following the contents of the booklet we are very likely to operate the gadget wrongly or damage it. While this approach is appreciated in the case of material goods and devices like VCD, TV etc., we forget or are indifferent to use a handbook already in existence for using the faculties of the human being.

Man is the most complex of all creations on this planet. Individual efforts at his improvement in some cases do take place. But many including organizations and institutions do not try seriously about it probably for the simple reason they believe such a manual does not exist.

In reality a well considered time tested set of guidelines for human excellence and happiness does exist. We don't call it a manual. It has been in existence for thousands of years in India which has a great heritage and wisdom. The scriptures contain this quintessence of guidelines for excellence. They contain principles of human conduct based on the realization of great sages who had nothing but the welfare of humanity at heart.

Of such scriptures the most important is the Bhagavad-Gita which holds the key to lift man from the worst type of depression to great heights of achievement in a convincing manner.

The Gita helps to effect a total transformation in his outlook and attitudes and capacity to overcome challenges of life. It explains in sufficient detail how to overcome depression, avoid stress, do one's duty with dedication, and attain human excellence. It stipulates beyond doubt what should be done and what should not be done to attain excellence. It also clearly indicates the influence of food on the quality of decision making and the thinking process to be developed. It gives the tool of meditation to avoid stress. It makes man a treasure worthy of making great contribution to the welfare of society and to himself.

Gita discusses various aspects of the art of man making. Management will benefit and grow if consistent efforts are made to imbibe the principles of human conduct and excellence laid down in this great scripture. If this is ignored, even if we producing probably a million Nobel laureates, economics and management will undoubtedly fail to ensure human happiness and prosperity with sustainability in all walks of life.

It is a welcome sign, a silver lining, that a few business schools have started realizing the relevance of this ancient scripture for human excellence. The world will witness faster and substantial progress if all business schools and institutions teach and imbibe the art of man making.

The focus has to be on the individual. Then the family, society, nation and the world will definitely progress. The benefits will be high quality of life, human happiness and prosperity with sustainability. The truth of this assertion is as certain as death. May the grace of the Lord be showered on all citizens and institutions of the world to imbibe this great, wonderful art of man making.

End of Vol.2